An Exalted Sky, Exulting

An Exalted Sky, Exulting

More Short Poems of Rumi,
by Coleman Barks, inspired by scholarly
work done by Ibrahim W. Gammard
and A. G. Rawan Farhadi

The Fons Vitae Rumi Series

FONS VITAE

First published in 2022 by
Fons Vitae
49 Mockingbird Valley Drive
Louisville, KY 40207
http://www.fonsvitae.com
Email: fonsvitaeky@aol.com

Library of Congress Control Number: 2022950582
ISBN 978-1941610-572

Very special thanks to my dear friend Zuleikha and my daughter
in law, Kelley Barks for helping in the preparation of this volume.
Thank you, Anne Ogden for thorough proofreading, and thanks
also to Gesa Gouverneur for layout and design.

Printed in Canada

For Robert Bly

Contents

An Introduction

It has not been my intention (though I may have said so elsewhere) to put Rumi's poetry into the American free verse tradition. My intention is to put Rumi's poetry into an American idiom that is clear and simple enough to let the mystery of identity come through with the power and the essence that it has at its core. The humor, the soul-surrendering love, the companionship that is contained in his friendship with Shams Tabris, THAT mystery, certainly, cannot be said, but it can be felt.

The blessings that have come to me from the work on the Poems of Rumi are many. The blessings began on a day in June in 1976 when Robert Bly handed me a copy of the scholarly translations of A.J. Arberry, *The Mystical Poems of Rumi*, University of Chicago Press, 1965, and said, "These poems need to be released from their cages," by which he meant they need to be rephrased out of their stiff English translation idiom into the more fluid, accessible language of the American free verse tradition begun by Walt Whitman and continued into the 20th century by many American Poets. Many of these were friends of Robert and would make appearances at the Great Mother Conference, where Robert was giving me this delightful, and blessed, writing assignment which, it turns out, I have continued working on for, at least, forty-seven years! There's no end in sight.

I feel certain that I will die still working on my "version" of Rumi's great masterpiece, the six volumes of the *Masnavi*. It began that June afternoon in Ely, Minnesota. I will continue on, blessedly, this beautiful Spring day, April 16th, 2021. This "work," or blessed play and astonishing relaxation, has brought me many friends. The poet Bill Stafford gave the first Rumi collection, *Open Secret*, a Pushcart Prize. Bill became a good friend and certainly a glorious blessing in my life. Thank you, Bill. He's gone now, as is Galway and Jim Dickey, and dear Donald Hall.

The Rumi "re-workings," by which I mean mostly *The Essential Rumi*, have been translated into twenty-six languages including

Finish, Gaelic, Russian, and Indonesian. They have sold something like 4 1/2 million copies worldwide! A phenomenon in publishing. The greatest mystical poet who ever lived. His poems continue to sprout in and nourish the imaginations of readers as they have for the last eight hundred years, continuously! It's a very lively friendship, the blessing of his poetry, and certainly the source of my deepest gratitude and enthusiasm.

In this new collection of Rumi poems, many have been inspired and reworked from *The Quatrains of Rumi*, translated by Ibrahim W. Gammard and A. G. Rawan Farhadi (San Rafael, CA: Sufi Dari Books, 2008). I want to recommend and celebrate the magnificent scholarship of Gammard and Farhadi, who are scholars of the purest ray, thorough and impeccable, precise and generous.

Their care and thorough devotional attention are evident throughout that indispensable text. Ibrahim Gammard and Rawan Farhadi's magnificent edition of *The Quatrains of Rumi* should be in everyone's library. It is a model of devoted scholarship. Their love of the poetry is apparent in everything they do. Their notes on the poems are words to absorb and be nourished by. These Notes are layered and mystical. They understand from the inside out Rumi's central ecstatic insight: that just to be in a body and conscious is cause for rapture. Their understanding of Rumi's poetry is experiential. The authority they bring to this text is whole and gorgeous. They feel the music of the language and they communicate that subtlety with consummate skill.

I am also profoundly grateful to Masood Khalili for the inspiration I have received from his magnificent quatrains. The son of the poet-laureate of Afghanistan, Masood himself is both a revered warrior and poet.

A Note About My Comments and the Title

My comments will be found in *italics* throughout the volume.

A note about the title: behind my choosing such a hyperbolic title is the Emily Dickinson poem #143 in the Franklin edition, page 186:

> Exultation is the going
> Of an inland soul to sea–
> Past the Houses–
> Past the Headlands–
> Into deep Eternity.
>
> Bred as we, among the mountains,
> Can the sailor understand
> The divine intoxication
> Of the first League out from Land?

The exalted/exulting hyperbole (and repetition) is an expression of the poet's "divine intoxication" that the sailor/speaker feels as he/she leaves the normal world and heads out into the unknown: that crossover that is the mystery and subject of this poem. The sailor/speaker's going-out from the normal, the reasonable, into the source, the soul, the ocean of what is praised. That "going" is the source of the exuberance (the hyperbole). Hyperbolic language is appropriate for such a crossover.

My mother taught Bible studies and her favorite verse contained the word "exalted," a word she loved.

> Psalm 46:10: Be still and know that I am God. I will be exalted among the heathen, I will be exalted in the earth.

Coleman Barks

The Poems

The good news comes: And He is
with you, wherever you are, (Qur'an 57:4)

Bits of light from that
appear in the heart.

You grieve because you do not know who you are.
When you do know, you will be filled with those
lightpoint sparks.

> *Bawa Muhaiyaddeen said to those who came to his room, "You are these light points in my eyes."*

Since I've been away from you,
I only know how to weep
Like a candle, melting is who I am.
Like a harp, any sound I make is music.

I want to leap out of this personality,
and sit apart from that leaping,
with the long-faced llamas.

Instead I become this portrait
of me being carefully painted by the wind
in the tall space inside of me.

Each flower, the water's face.

Something opens our wings.
Something makes boredom and hurt
disappear.

> *There is a flipping of the moth-become-candle image, here where the harp becomes music becomes David Darling playing his cello in an English meadow with two llamas looking over the fence at the other end of the meadow, Devon, early morning. He's still very much alive.*

At dawn today, the full moon appeared,
gazing at me.

Then like a hawk it stooped, and picked me up,
and carried me across the sky.

I looked down at myself. I was no more!
Through this grace my body became my soul.

The secret of how spirit reveals itself came to me. The nine levels became one.
My ship sunk in the ocean.

I became the sea!

None of this would have happened
if I had not met Shams Tabriz.

> *I'm doing a writing assignment that Robert Bly told me to, on or about June 5th, 1976. It's November 16th, 2022 now. Robert's birthday is December 23rd. He died last on November 21st, 2021.*

Try to hear the poems as part of a conversation
between self and soul, you and I, in a deep communion.
The "you" might be called many things, "the one
who floods the private sanctuary I've built," "someone
sober," also the "I" is very elusive. Both are
undefined, really.
"Nothing in this existence but that existence."

The soul is called "the secret core in everyone,"
"that presence within," "your loving," "the Friend,"
and "the center," sometimes in the same poem.
The soul is identical with "a secret turning in us
that makes the universe turn."
A union, though, (of self and soul) can happen.
"love mixing with spirit"
The great spaciousness that comes then has a name:
Shams Tabriz.
The unsayable mystery, though, is always that
of "to die before you die."
So the talking (*sohbet*) keeps opening out.
There is no solving the riddle of this conversation.

Some Thoughts on Rumi's Quatrains

Quatrains arose from many different situations. This one, from the milling-around of the crowd as it moved into the area where Rumi was to give the evening discourse. The question arose as to where was the place of honor. Where does "the Friend" sit, and who is the Friend?

The secret you told, tell again.
There is always a secret that must be told,
and when it is, the two go wandering off
together. That wandering is the clearest direction.
The door that opens then is like "the night ocean
filled with glints of light.
We are the space between the fish
and the moon, while we sit here together.
This companionship opens them out of
quietness into "long stories and singing."
What is real is this friendship, and their voices
rising into the dome!
A door opens. It's the friends we've been
looking for!
The moth becomes the candle
and the candle melts into music.
Do not think all this is unconscious.
It is rather like a pot of water when a thousand tiny bubbles
come up to tell the chef it is about to come to full-boil.

Commenting on the Unseen Rain poems.

Rumi speaks of two human impulses: to drink long and deep, and to sober up too soon. To give in to surrender, and to return to order. Both are strong and deeply human.

Do not presume that the earth
around you, this world, do not think all this
is unconscious. Rather, it is like a rabbit
awake with eyes half closed. It is like a pot of water
when a thousand tiny bubbles begin to come up
to tell the chef it is about to make full-boil.

> *The French, with their love of cuisine, have a name for this stage of the cooking process, but I have forgotten what it is. This pre-boil stage of consciousness is an important preliminary for Rumi, essential to the soul's survival and continued growth.*

My head, my mind, you are a synapse
within a series of reasonable, measured synapses.
My body, you are a wonder set within other wonders,
threaded through with other wonders.
My heart, your desiring hides within a longing
within a deep aura of love.
Soul, your joy lies within yourself, within another joy,
within the whole, which is also a great joy.

> *Head, body, heart, and soul, those are the four arms of the physical that make up the musical language of this quatrain. As I understand Gammard and Farhadi, the editors and translators of* The Quatrains of Rumi, *there are seven areas of physical and psychic experience being expressed here (in #1668), and, somehow, the sound of the poem flows through all seven components (the impulse to let go and the impulse that recognizes beauty are part of the mix). The musical language-dance, they say, is somehow what is being talked about.*

The Friend says, I am beautiful,
so make yourself beautiful by
living in this friendship.

If you want to be a source of gemstones,
let your chest become an ocean.

Here Rumi is responding to a saying of Muhammad.

I don't usually disagree with a saying of Muhammad. But here is one that I do:
This world is a prison for the believer. (I don't understand.)
I see no prison. But who he did not say, *This world is a prison for the servants.*
Servants and *believers* are very different.
"Prison" I understand as a way of thinking, a closing-in.
When that happens, tell your friend and be done with it.
Don't think: how can I be so small-minded
with this one I am close to?
Your soul will know all about these things
whether you say it or not.

This depth of being alone with God
is more than I could feel and
know in a thousand lifetimes.

This freedom inside this solitude
is more than could ever be
given to me
in all the kingdoms by all the saints of the world,
more than anywhere, anytime!
More than this and more than that!

It is the truest and most singular.
It is my gift to you. It's all I have!
This depth and this freedom.
Here it is, contained in a quatrain.

When I met that very beautiful man, Hazrat Chelebi, he was traveling with the dervishes. They were doing a Sema in Atlanta at the World Congress Center. He is a direct descendent of Rumi's friend and chief disciple, Husam Chelebi. He sat me down and said, "NOW! What religion are you?" I put both hands in the air, palms up in the "Who knows?" gesture. "Good!" he said, "Love is the religion and the universe is the book!" Then he turned away. That's all that needs be said. He gave me a facsimile copy of Rumi's Masnavi. *I will happily spend the rest of my life doing a version of that book.*

I am the guest of this music.
You are the life of these friends,
the soul of this music, swaying ocean-center.
Let this wide music field be filled with your being

Every thought I've ever had inside a mosque,
or near the kaaba, going around that,
saying "I am here. I am here."
Every thought was praising you!

I understand that so clearly now
And also in the wine tavern, there too,

The connectivity through the eyes
that we have in such moments, all that exchange
was healing me. That was the cure that
I have been longing for. The being healed
was YOU! It all grew from you!

Lord, show us how to be completely
and truly human. Let us be known
for the deep friendship in our hearts.
Let it be in that first light, where we feel
the deepest joy of being human.
Show us the core of that joy!

We are fully aware in the tavern
where we know the moth-nature of our being.

The way we circle around each other
in the mosque, in the church,
in all the holiest places.
We coil and curl over and around each other
like snakes.

David Darling once set up a wooden chair in an English meadow, in Devon, and played, improvising on the cello, his great heart out into the fall morning air. On the other side of the field, two llamas stood watching and listening with their long sweet faces leaning just barely over the fence at the other end of the field. Thank you, David, for this moment in my memory so spontaneously devised, and for all the glorious moments you gave us.

In love, there is one step, then another,
the most real being the step-over
from pre-existence into existence.

You think that in non-existence
you see many different beings. Not so.
Rub your eyes and look again.

In non-existence, there is only not-ness,
annihilation-in-God, everywhere only that.

I am not I, but if I were for one moment
I would stir up this world of dust particles
and mix it all together in a cloud.

If I were that *one*, who I am,
who has uprooted his heart from his personal
limits, I would be like a tree lifted out of the earth
with all its roots exposed like its limbs and its leaves.

Hearing the answer is not nothing
but everything, although:
The Inuit Shaman, Orpingalik,
Once, when asked what a
poem was, said, when
the great mystery, that of
which words cannot be said or
known, but only can be lived within,
when that tries to take
a public form, it comes
to mind in one person's
head and so is, for a
moment, somewhere
here and now, in one passing.

Now. The time for discipline has come.
Observe Ramadan. For a few days hold back
from even mentioning, or thinking about
the bowl for eating hot lentil soup
or the jar for keeping springwater cool.

Wander around this empty tablecloth,
begging. Let the cotton loosen from
the pod that holds it in the cotton field
where it is getting ready to become this
tablecloth.

I have only really known the discipline of doing Ramadan once. That was in Konya in 1984. Never has lentil soup tasted so good as it did for those two weeks every night at 8 pm and the water, from heaven.

Every floating dust-mote in the air
close around us here, and out
over the high desert,
and all the mountains, are just as distracted
and amazed as we are. Each of us,
whether we are personally happy or sad, we all
feel the incomparable joy of the great sun
that is here inside us, now.
That is our reality now.

Non-existence is preparing more tasty experiences for you.
Tray on tray are coming down in layers of abundance.

Many of Rumi's quatrains are glosses on passages from the Qur'an. This one, 84:19, "You will travel from stage to stage," combined with 5:114, when Jesus prays and a table comes with trays of food from heaven.

This one wanders the night-town
Because of a different wine.
You religious police, don't scold this
friend of mine.
The more you scold, the drunker
he will become.
The jug he drank from
is empty and spinning
on top of his head.

As the meeting hall fills up one night, and everyone is finding their seat, the question arises, "Where does the friend sit" and "Who is the Friend?"

> *Rumi's answer is, "Whatever makes you happy, whatever makes you sad, your whole existence, whatever you call those, everything, all this, is the Friend!"*

Sometimes it's a separation that wants to turn away from this world and leave. Other times, it's the deep inward joy of union. The feel of the self and God together. How odd and sad it is that on the white tablet where everything has already happened it says:

This on one day, that on another.
The fire that tries and wants to burn it all up
and the union that claims it
is wholly ours.
This is the condition called Majesty.

Now that your kindness has won out, this is how it is:
There are no mean-spririted people anywhere.
No worries about more and less.
Everyone has become a king.
Majesty is everywhere.
No beggars. Just kings.
Impossible, but, it is so.
We *feel* the *majesty* everywhere!

At dawn today, the full moon appeared,
gazing at me.

Then like a hawk it stooped, and picked me up,
and carried be across the sky.

I looked down at myself. I was no more!
Through this grace my body became my soul.

The secret of how spirit reveals itself came to me.
The nine levels became one.
My ship sunk in the ocean.

I became the sea.
None of this would have happened
if I had not met Shams Tabriz.

The world's millwheel may seem to have slowed and *stopped working*, but the lover is still fully involved with his millwork.

When others seem sad and expecting the worse,
the lover is bright and busy and optimistic.

Show the lover all the places
where the candles have gone out.

He'll contrive to light a thousand
in each of the places where there was a single flame.

A lover may seem alone,
but he's not.
His friend
is there close-by his head.

Wine is always bubbling up inside a lover.

The lover has no use for future things.
He knows how quickly those can change and not happen.

The lover is interested in the lively horse
that starts out quickly! One touch,
and he's gone!
The roughness of the road is not a problem.
And don't give bland food to a lover.

He wants the complex taste of the finest red wine.
Lovers make the most discerning vintners!

In Shams Tabriz you will find a heart
that is sometimes completely clear and sober
and at the same time wildly excited.

How does this doubleness happen?
THAT is his secret. Let it become yours.

You birds, who have left your cages,
I want to ask one thing: Come here!
Show your faces! Tell me who you are!

Your ship has sunken in this place. Rise up
and slip out of the hand that caught you.
Be fish again! Do you feel the fire
that now is catching in you? Do you see the light
and feel the rising wind?
You died and were born in one moment.
As a Hindu, or a Turk; it doesn't matter.

You met Shams and were born as something else.
Let the veils fall off and your selves become
new kinds of friends for Shams Tabriz.
That's what you most truly are!

Dawn. And it's the full moon, not the sun,
that comes to look at me, and get my attention,
sleeping, napping through this morning. It comes to me
this flight carrying me off to another landscape,
another world where I am NOT. And more:
The scene changes to a sea. The sea surges,
the sea of my sleeping being that is carried off
to the hawk-moon's nest. Thus it happened,
and so it befell. The sea foamed up with an edge
of foam-flakes, and something took form. Something
became the spirit in that sea, and this time,
the essence of majesty, which is Shams Tabriz.

I have never felt that this world is a prison. All I see is an
exalted sky, a freedom, exulting. If someone pisses on my hands,
I immediately forgive him. Thank you, sir.
So, bravo for me!
You wonder when I hide myself away for a long time.
That's because I did not know who I was.
But now I see.
What surprising beauty!
I am like a pearl one finds in a latrine, down in the dung.
I had imagined myself free of all that.
Hardly. No. Not at all.

I am not the head of anything. Just wandering through,
causing trouble. I am the least respectable one here
tonight. No. None of that is true.
I am a brush in the hand of the one who is painting
this ongoing, soul-making, empty universe.
I do not know who I am
or what I am doing at the
moment.

He does know, though, that he is in space and time. And that he is profoundly ignorant of what he is doing here. I love his admission, and celebration, of ignorance in his world view. See Niffari, for whom ignorance is the central concept. I have a clear memory of an actual caravanserai in Turkey. It, an enormous empty space, with room enough for several caravans and all their animals. It was a little west of Konya.

I say to my heart, Not again, not another love,
all that affliction. Then the friend, who is my heart, says,
Listen to you. I am bringing you new wonder and great new
beauty. This hesitation is your pride. Hesitation and aloofness are
always PRIDE! *Remember this.*

Remember? The soul-bird rises in flight. The ocean fills on its wide, smooth floor with pearls once more.
The salt marsh grows as sweet as fresh pasture. An ordinary piece of gravel becomes a ruby in your hand.
Body becomes soul. Now your eyes are raining tears. Lightning lights the sky around your house. Do you know why the lovers' eyes are clouding over?

The moon slides behind a cloudbank. Rain comes in big cold drops, the way we love for it to.
The earth is washed clean and clear, like a stone ruin.

We are safe in this ship with our captain, Noah.
He knows these rising waters well. The six directions dissolve into each other:
up-down, North-East-South-West, inside-outside.

An orchard of date trees begins to grow beneath
the surface of the ground.
Seeds break open into a new plantation.
The live, wet, root starts on its way
to becoming a fresh green branch.
And now, a fire of dry branches makes a laughing sound. Something closes my mouth, and I say to myself, "You have done it again!" "You are drunk and too near the edge of the roof."
Try to understand your confusion.

Be still and know what is inside you
that keeps bringing you to this dangerous edge.

Now the king leading this string of camels puts me in front. He wets his ring with his mouth and presses it on a document. Now he puts that ring for a knocker on my door.

As blood becomes semen and enters an egg to become a new human being, so that human being must die to become clear and more like a soul.

Let this poem end here, but let my voice continue to be heard
over the rooftops. Let me move above this commotion I have made.

This new Spring poem is the last installment on my work completing Robert Bly's assignment, which was to put the Cambridge translations (of Arberry and Nicholson) into a more appropriate idiom, that of American free verse. Robert told me, "These poems need to be released from their cages." For fifty-six years I have tried to do that! I hope the sky of their escaping truly is "exulting."

My chest is full and breathing in your school.
The doctor says I have a fever. That's from you.

I have given up all he told me to,
except the kindness and the wild life
of your presence.
Those two I keep with me here in my heart.

His answer:
Whatever makes you happy.
Whatever makes you grieving and distracted.
Whatever you call those, which is everything,

All this is the Friend, your existence and
your non-existence.
Nothing gets solved about
the question of where to sit.

My salamander soul feels so at home
in this fire of longing. You are the wine
that takes me into sleep and dream.

Why the salamander is associated with
living comfortably inside a fire, I do not know.
Who first made that strong connection?

We wish we could see those who are
blessed. Others wish this too. Now it happens
that by our laughing playfulness, our
longing has removed all reason, every conventional
practice, and whatever else there was.

A warm, rainy, spring day.
This is how it feels when friends get together,
when friend refreshes friend as flowers do
each other, in a spring rain.

A beautifully clear haiku, celebrating again how it is with friends, in a spring rain. I love this rubai of Rumi for how it recapitulates the work of the Japanese haiku (see The Essential Haiku, *ed. by Robert Hass) into the new era of play that the American short poem opened up.*

My heart is the instrument I play,
like the rebab or the cello, or the reed flute, in tune with my
voice. So then when I found my heart had found another,
I kept repeating foolishly, idiotically, But that's my friend.
It's foolish to think that just one instrument is yours,
and only one.

This bird is free of its cage.
This cage, released of its bird.
Both so empty, so ecstatic,
that they let fragrance come
through this song, eternity in tears.

They will say, in the coming years, I wish we could have been alive when Rumi was, so we could have been his friends and heard his words and his poems as he spoke them. You have that very companionship now. Don't waste this chance! Look at him as the souls of the prophets are seeing him. Not with the eyes you have now.

I love this—
how we are together.
God has given me this friendship!
I was so bored with myself.
I wanted someone I could turn toward,
as a prayer rug points to Mecca.
Someone to turn my face to.
Do you understand what I am saying about boredom?
You do.
I have a friend now
who understands what I'm saying!

The one who looked down at us from the roof
yesterday, from the porch up there,
that one is a spirit, or something radiantly
inward. Anyone who has lived without knowing
such a face has not lived. When one says one is
awake without knowing *such a one*,
that is proof that one has not become conscious.

The Friend says, Let the beauty of this friendship
be your beauty. The source of sweetness is a nowhere.
Make yourself a place to live
there where there is no where.

When I step over into death,
I will give a shout into non-existence,
so that the emptiness itself
will be astonished, saying,
Nowhere in this world have I seen someone so wild
in their love
for what is, and what isn't.

No matter where I went, all I saw was SKY!
I was no longer myself! The ocean surged and fell back.
A voice came out of it.

And every fleck of ocean foam became
a different form and a sign from that
ultimate creativity.
But I am sure of this:

That NONE of this would have happened,
no secret of the eternal revelation would have been
disclosed, without the coming here of the
crowning grace of Shams Tabriz!

NOW! You birds who have left your cages,
I want to ask you to do one thing: Come HERE!
Show your faces!
Tell me who you are!

Your ship has sunk in this place.
Rise up! Slip out of the hand that caught you!

Be fish again!
Do you feel the fire that has caught in you?
Do you see the light? And feel the rising wind?

You died and were reborn in one moment.
Be a Hindu, or a Turk.
It doesn't matter.

You have met Shams and been born as something else.

Let the veils fall off and each of you become
a new kind of friend for Shams Tabriz.

That's what you most truly ARE!

It was a wild new dawn when that full moon
came and took me with its beauty
into the crowning grace of a Friendship with Shams!

Ocean Foam

And now comes in to this, the squirrel I saw at the corner of Oakland and Stanton Way, being lifted by a hawk by his shoulder-skin and carried off, looking back at me as though to say, Can you help me? I'm being carried to his nest of saw-tooth moonchicks who will eat me alive and turn this into a bloody mess for whatever's next in this afternoon stew, this holy gumbo. The flight that afternoon carried me out of my personality into the sea-surge of a dream where my friend, the poet Galway Kinnell, is pointing me with lifted arm into a cave entrance, over which it says in block letters made of fire: RASA SHAMSI TABRIZ, which means, The Essence of Shams Tabriz, which is what is ALWAYS being disclosed in the poetry of Rumi: Sun becoming moon becoming foam-bubbles in an ocean where saints are meditating and a rough wooden chair waits for Shams to sit down. I'll try to draw a picture.

It's the central furniture of this most luminous dream I've ever had.

The chair was on the edge of an abyss, The foam-bubble wave of the world being changed into spirit, as he was by the hawk-moon Sun of Shams Tabriz.

Eyes that don't see the beauty,
Do they make the beauty less?
What people say, does that matter to the lover?
We move along this love-road quickly,
with some agility in our step.

One of us draws up lame.
Do we all stop?

Your existence and your non-existence are entirely
THAT which makes you happy, which makes you cry,

All this is the Friend.

Only your eyes do not see the beauty. Otherwise, head to foot you are living inside the one you ask about. (This quatrain was spoken by Rumi in answer to the question, Who is the Friend?)

It is amazing, unbelievable really, that we know so much about incidents in Rumi's life, like the one that his quatrain came from. It came from a meeting in the king's palace by special invitation, all of the local dignitaries were there: the great scholars, the recluses, the travelers from other countries. When Rumi's group arrived, Rumi is asked to settle the question of protocol...who should sit in the place of honor in the meeting hall? Husam Chelabi had arrived early at the meeting a little before Rumi's group. He enters and goes up to the raised dias and sits there. Other prominent men from the community join him, so that when Rumi enters there is no room on the sofa, the extended seat where the teachers sit. Husam joins him there, as do some others from the dais, the most proud, though, the hypocrites, stay in there falsely exalted seats. Some discussion follows. Many very subtle scholarly minds are there. It is like a library of religious science. They pose the problem, in this present situation where is the seat of honor? One says, in the middle of the raised platform, the traditional place of the teacher. According to those who practice spiritual withdrawal, it is in the corner of the lodge, the saviya *still another: among some Sufis is it just there by the raised platform where people remove their shoes. They turn to Rumi, what is your custom? Where is the doorway? Where is the most honored seat? Where are we? Each one of us? Where am I? Rumi answers, "Wherever the Friend is." "But where is the friend? someone shouts. This is the big question in a sufi* Kanaqah, *the one you ask with your whole life.*

Rumi speaks this poem:

A group stands up and begins to turn, the *sama* becomes so passionate that many of the prominent citizens and subtle scholars tear their expensive robes and keep on dancing, all pretention abandoned.

Even in Hell, if you are there,
I will not want to leave.
And if I find myself in heaven
without you, those wide fields
will be confining to my breathing-heart.

Shams is speaking this poem.

When a poem comes in the midst of my talking,
I feel an opening in me. I begin to say
the secret meanings. Some people get quiet
when they hear those. Rumi gets overwhelmed
sometimes in that way. Others are stunned by the
lack of clear meaning. More of that (happens where)
People have a right to object to anything I say.
These words come from a vast place. They sound pretentious perhaps,
When Muhammad spoke the Qur'an, his words came because they
had to. There was an urgency, a searching need. My speech
is not talk like that. These words are from so high up, if you look at them,
your hat will fall off. People hear me and say, "He claims to be so
great." Which is true, certainly. What's wrong with the truth?
In other words, I am so great! And so God-like!
I don't deny it. I claim it.

Even though you cannot see the end
of the road -- it may be it has no end.
Still, start out. Watching others on the way
is how cowards live their lives. This is for
those with a courageous heart. The true human
beings
who have moved beyond what the body
fears and what the body wants. THINK OF THAT!

Give up this fumbling with beads,
this chanting in the dark, shut temple.

Who do you think you are worshiping in here
all closed up?

Open your eyes.
Open the doors and go outside.
A man is plowing his field.
A mason
is breaking and laying stone for a path.

In rain and sunlight, covered with dust, the master
of creation works inside our work.

Leave your meditation practice.
Put away the incense and essential oil.

Get torn and exhausted in a day of physical work.
You will find that God
is working beside you.

*My son, Benjamin, does strenuous physical work each day.
He knows the truth of this poem well.*

I have not sung the song I came here to sing.
I have spent the time stringing
and unstringing my instrument.

The words are not right. The truth of my time
has not been said, only this
deep longing in my heart.

The blossom has not opened in the wind.
I have not seen his face,
nor heard his voice.

Only the sound of his footsteps on the dirt road
in front of my house.

I have spread the mat on the floor,
making a place for him to sit,

but I have not lit the lamp or asked him in.
I have lived my life hoping for this meeting,

but it has not happened yet.

This meeting!

We are the lazy lovers lying on our sides in the grass,
talking, napping. Generosity and grace have given
the earth itself saddles and good horses,
and a well-made wagon, so we can be carried along
in our sleep,
in our laziness, the way of those
cave companions. (Remember them?) We are like
those young men, and their dog, who slept
joyfully for centuries.

A Note for the End

I grew up on the campus of a boys' school, Baylor in Chattanooga. The school was on a hill overlooking the Tennessee River. A very beautiful place, Locust Hill. It was named for the grove of black locust trees there. At six years old, I was fascinated, obsessed, with maps. My favorite possession was a 1943 Rand McNally Atlas and Gazetteer. I looked through it so much that I (without meaning to) memorized all the capitals of all the countries in the world. It became known, on that hill, that I had this weird expertise. So it was continually tested. As I walked to the dining hall (I had every meal with four hundred people. Forty tables, ten to a table.) People would call out countries to me, and I would answer back the capital. Bulgaria! Sofia. Bhutan! Thimphu. Lithuania! Vilnius. I never missed. My perfect six/seven year old mind knew them all (I still do) and I knew that I knew. Finally, the great trickster, James Pennington, the Latin teacher, went down to his classroom in the basement of the chapel and found a country on his map that did not seem to have a capital. He called across the quadrangle, Cappadocia! I remember exactly where I was standing. By which bush. He said, "The look on your face named you." So from then on, on top of that hill, which was my entire world, my name was Cappadocia! Or Capp for short. There are still people in Chattanooga, who, when they see me will call out Cappadocia. Years later, I found out that the central city in that region of central Turkey is Iconium or Konya, where Rumi lived and is buried! I've been there many times. I am fascinated, too much perhaps, by synchronicities. They make such perfect sense.

This is surely Rumi's most frequently quoted quatrain:

Come, come, whoever you are,
wanderer, worshiper, lover of leaving,
it doesn't matter.
Ours is not a caravan of despair.
Come, even if you have broken your vow a thousand times.
Still come, and yet come again, Come.

This quatrain has long been associated with the Mevlevi order of Konya.

A Turkish version with English translation is in a glass case in the Rumi museum in Konya, along with a copy of the quatrains. There still remains, though, some doubt about the poem's authorship. It may not be by Rumi. A similar quatrain (I am told) is attributed to Abil Khayr (died 1049).

It seems appropriate that Rumi's most well-known and most-quoted poem may not be by him!

Reshad Field was perhaps most well-known for his beautiful reciting, with his wonderful singing voice, of this short, passionate, invitational poem. And come they do, by the thousands, every December to Konya. It is truly one of the great ecstatic gatherings on earth, December 17th, remembering Rumi's death, in 1273.

Not to be missed, by any lover of Rumi. Truly, Come! And yet again, Come!

A Rumi deathbed story: The day he died, December 17, 1273, there were rumblings of earthquakes in the region. "Be patient!" he called out. "You'll get your juicy morsel soon!" Implying the earth's hungry stomach was growling. December 17th is called his *Urs*, or wedding night, when he was revisited and returned to the presence of Shams.

Coleman Barks

A Tribute from an Afghan Warrior and Poet

Mountain to mountain can not reach but heart to heart can. Coleman Barks with his new book, *An Exalted Sky*, reaches to the hearts of those who believe that God is love and love is God. Coleman fills the souls of millions of people with the fragrances of the dawn-scented flowers of Rumi's poetry. Coleman amazingly rephrases Rumi's quatrains into beautiful English words. While selecting the quatrains of Rumi, Coleman is like a moth: kissing, caressing, smelling, and dancing around the eternal flame of love mingled with pain and peace, smile and tear, hope and fear, lament and laughter. Colman whispers to our hearts with a Divine message that through love we live forever—without it, we die every minute. Let me thank you, Coleman, on behalf of Rumi and millions of those who read your everlasting books. I am honored that my humble quatrains inspired your soft soul. Let us always keep the candle of love lit in our hearts and the sunrise of hope shine in our lives.

Masood Khalili